Intended For Greatness

Lessons from the Life of Solomon

Grant Crary

INTENDED FOR GREATNESS
LESSONS FROM THE LIFE OF SOLOMON
by Grant Crary

Copyright © 2019 Grant Crary. All rights reserved.
ISBN: 978-0-9982243-2-9

Cover design by David Crary

All scripture is taken from the New King James Version. Copyright © 1982 by Thomas Nelson, Inc. All rights reserved. Used by permission.

Printed in the United States of America.

Published by:
Fairdale Publishing
www.fairdalepublishing.com

No part of this publication may be reproduced, stored in a retrieval system, or transmitted in any form, or by any means, electronic, mechanical, including photocopy, recording, or by any informational storage and retrieval system, without the prior, written permission of the publisher. Please direct permission requests and other correspondences to Fairdale Publishing (fairdalepublishing.com).

Dedication

This book is dedicated to my wife, Jillian, who has been my friend and companion throughout our life together. Her wisdom, kindness, encouragement, and love for the Lord are a priceless blessing.

CONTENTS

Introduction . . . . *vii*

Chapter 1. God's Appearances to Solomon. 3

Chapter 2. Promises 11

Chapter 3. God's Perspective 23

Chapter 4. Solomon's Wealth 31

Chapter 5. Solomon's Wisdom. 39

Chapter 6. Wisdom, and the Fear of the Lord 49

Chapter 7. Staying on Course 59

Chapter 8. Solomon and David. 67

Chapter 9. Solomon's Legacy 77

INTRODUCTION

A significant portion of the Bible is devoted to King Solomon. He is referred to in thirteen books in all, the account of his life being principally covered in the books of 1 Kings and 2 Chronicles. In fact, Jesus Himself referred to Solomon, declaring that the Queen of Sheba, who traveled "from the ends of the earth to hear the wisdom of Solomon" will rise in judgement on this generation because they failed to listen to One who was greater than Solomon.

Solomon was a man of considerable accomplishments and he wrote several books of the Bible, namely Ecclesiastes, Song of Solomon, and most of the book of Proverbs. He was responsible for substantial building projects and accumulated enormous wealth. His wisdom, knowledge, and understanding are legendary, and there has never been a wiser man than him on the face of the earth, other than the Lord Himself. Yet in spite of his great wisdom, Solomon made some very unwise decisions, which ultimately led to his kingdom being divided, early in the reign of his son and successor.

Solomon's life contains many lessons that we can apply to our own lives, and we will discuss them in this book. Therefore, the book is written in a manner that presents the lessons by topics, rather than a chronological discourse on his life. We will see the extent of wisdom that God can grant to us, His great love for us, and also how wrong decisions can have serious consequences.

Solomon was a man who was loved by God. He was also blessed with a wonderful example to follow in his father, David. He had so much going for him, and if ever a man was destined to be great, it had to be Solomon. Sadly, although Solomon became great by every standard of worldly achievement, he was disobedient to God's word and he paid the price for that disobedience.

Although Solomon began his reign very well, later in his life he fell into idolatry. Because he was a leader, his sin affected not only him but also those under his leadership, in this case, the entire nation. It would appear that Solomon came to regret his bad decisions and did return to the Lord. However, he could not undo the consequences. It should serve as an example and reminder to us that our decisions have a resulting outcome, either for good or for bad.

I trust that this look into Solomon's life will encourage you to pursue the things that Solomon did right, and consequently, to grow continually closer to the God who loved him and blessed him in great abundance. May these blessings be yours also.

Intended For
Greatness

ONE

GOD'S APPEARANCES TO SOLOMON

Do you know someone who has been privileged to have the Lord appear to them? Not many of us do, because it is rare. As far as we know, the Lord did not appear to some of the great men of the Bible, such as David, even though he was a man after God's own heart (Acts 13:22). Because of David's walk with God, he actually became the yardstick by which all of the kings of Judah were measured, and over and over, we read how a particular king lived or did not live like David. For example, we read that King Josiah, "Did what was right in the sight of the Lord, and walked in all the ways of his father, David." (2 Kings 22:2). And yet it seems that the Lord did not actually appear to David, and other righteous men and women as well, although it is certain that they had some wonderful experiences in His presence.

However, the Lord did appear to David's son, Solomon, on not one but two occasions. We should not interpret this to mean that Solomon's walk with God was superior to that of David, but a wonderful privilege that was granted to him. The first was shortly after his ascension to the throne, (1 Kings 3:4-15 and 2 Chronicles 1:6-12). Solomon had gone to Gibeon to offer sacrifices, and the Lord appeared to him in a dream during the night with an amazing offer. God said to Solomon, "Ask! What shall I give you?" It is certainly amazing that God would make such a blanket offer to someone, but He knows our hearts and how we shall choose. He knew that Solomon would choose well. We shall look at what Solomon requested and God's response to him.

The Bible records that Solomon asked for wisdom, knowledge, and understanding in order to govern God's people effectively. This request greatly pleased the Lord. We should ask ourselves, how was it that a nineteen-year-old would have such a perception of the real values in life that he would request these qualities? If we were to ask many modern teenagers what he or she would like, the answer would probably involve material things…cars, travel, wealth, electronics, position. So why did Solomon value wisdom above all other things that God could give to him?

The answer may be found in the book of Proverbs. The first nine chapters of Proverbs are quite different from the remainder of the book, and we find the instruction in these chapters frequently being addressed to, "My son," a phrase which occurs fourteen times. For example, Proverbs 1:8 says, "My son, hear the instruction of your father, and do not forsake the law of your mother," indicating that both parents were involved in the training of their son. It is possible that this could be Solomon writing to his son Rehoboam who succeeded him, but seeing that Rehoboam's mother was an Amorite it would seem more likely that Solomon was recording the instructions given to him by own parents, David and Bathsheba.

David himself was a very wise man, and one to whom God gave great insights. Little is known about the nature of Bathsheba, but her grandfather was a counsellor to David and also an exceptionally wise man. His name was Ahithophel and we are told that when one went to him for counsel, it was like inquiring at "the oracle of God" (2 Samuel 16:23). Unfortunately, he later turned against David and his end was disastrous, but nevertheless, the wisdom that he possessed was probably passed on to his children and grandchildren.

In order to understand what Solomon regarded as being important in life, we can consider what he wrote about wisdom. Over and over again in these early chapters of Proverbs, and indeed throughout his writings, we read about the value and importance of wisdom. In fact, Chapter Eight and most of Chapter Nine, are devoted entirely to wisdom. A few of the passages that extol the value of wisdom are:

- Proverbs 2:10 When wisdom enters your heart… discretion will preserve you.

- Proverbs 3:13 Happy is the man who finds wisdom…all the things you can desire cannot compare with her.

- Proverbs 4:7 Wisdom is the principal thing; therefore, get wisdom…

- Proverbs 7:4 Say to wisdom, "You are my sister…"

When the Lord gave Solomon the extraordinary opportunity to ask for whatever he wanted, Solomon had been well grounded in the value of wisdom. He must have had a teachable heart and a love for the things of God because when faced with this important decision, he made an outstanding choice. His request pleased the Lord, so much so that He also promised Solomon other things that he not requested. One of the things that God promised held a condition. The other promises were unconditional, meaning that there was no requirement placed on Solomon for their fulfillment. Here is what God promised unconditionally:

- A wise and understanding heart, greater than anyone before him and anyone who would come after him.

- Riches and honor above any other king in his time.

The promise that held a condition was that the Lord would give Solomon a long life. The condition to this promise was that Solomon must walk in God's ways, keeping His statutes and commands like David his father did.

If we fast forward to the end of Solomon's life, we can see that God kept His promises. Solomon was indeed gifted with exceptional wisdom, knowledge, and understanding. He was sought out by the leaders of other nations, such as the Queen of Sheba, who traveled perhaps as far as 2,000 miles to meet

Solomon and to see for herself whether what she had heard about him was true. She came to ask hard questions of him, and there was no question that she posed that Solomon could not answer. So great was his wisdom and wealth that she declared that it exceeded all that she had been told (1 Kings 10:7).

The wisdom and insights that God gave to Solomon truly were remarkable. We are told that he could lecture on a wide variety of subjects. He was an expert on trees, animals, birds, reptiles, and fish. He spoke three thousand proverbs and wrote one thousand and five songs (1 Kings 4:32-33). Solomon also had an excellent business sense, including how to conduct foreign trade, resulting in his kingdom becoming exceptionally wealthy. God had said that Solomon's wisdom would exceed that of any other person throughout history (other than the Lord Jesus), and certainly this promise has been kept.

However, as we noted, there was one promise from God that carried with it a condition. This was the promise of a long life, and the condition was that Solomon must walk in God's ways. Solomon began well, but later in his life, he turned to idolatry. He married many wives from surrounding nations, and they had brought their religious practices with them. Solomon must have allowed his wives to continue in these practices (worshiping false gods), and in time his wives turned his own heart after them too (1 Kings 11:4). Solomon's life was consequently shortened instead of being lengthened, and he died at the age of fifty-nine. In Ecclesiastes 4:13, he wrote of "...an old and foolish king who will be admonished no more." Most likely, he was referring to himself, as he realized the terrible mistake he had made.

Let us now look at the second time that God appeared to Solomon, which we read about in 1 Kings 9:1-9. This took place after he had completed his major building projects, twenty-four years into his reign. God spoke regarding both Solomon and of the nation of Israel. For Solomon, He promised that "the throne of his kingdom would be established forever," and that he would "not fail to have a man on the throne of Israel." These wonderful promises were conditional upon Solomon walking before God like David his father, keeping God's statutes and judgements. We know that some years later, Solomon would fail badly in this regard. In fact, God had specifically warned Solomon about turning to idolatry, and yet that is precisely what he did.

There are four important lessons that we should learn from God's appearances and messages to Solomon.

(1) The first lesson is that God keeps His promises. Even though Solomon was not faithful to God, he did not lose his great wisdom or his riches. God was angry at Solomon for his disobedience, but there were no conditions attached to the promises of wisdom and wealth. God kept His word, in spite of the provocation, even though the promises were exceptional. The wisdom and understanding that God gave to Solomon have been unparalleled, and his riches were astonishing.

(2) The fulfilment of promises may not be automatic. Most promises that God gives us are conditional upon our walking in obedience and in a right relationship with Him. For example, a promise of entering into a certain ministry could only be possible if we exhibit the right character.

Otherwise, we would fail in that ministry. Also, we cannot be passive regarding a promise. When Daniel realized that the seventy years of exile, as prophesied by Jeremiah, was over he began to earnestly pray for the Lord to move to fulfill the promise that He would bring the people back to Jerusalem and Judea. Daniel did not sit back and say, "Praise the Lord, it is going to happen!" Instead, he prayed and fasted. Daniel knew that he had to be actively involved for the fulfillment to be realized.

(3) We need to pay heed to warnings. At both appearances, God warned Solomon to walk in His ways, and even specifically warned him about idolatry. If God gives us a warning, it is because He knows that we have a weakness in that particular area of our lives. We need to earnestly pray that He will keep us from being unfaithful, because no matter how good are our intentions, we have the propensity to fall.

We see an example of this in the life of another king named Asa. Asa was a good man who did many righteous things. One day, when he was returning from a great victory in battle, he was met by a prophet who said, "The Lord is with you while you are with Him. If you seek Him, He will be found by you; but if you forsake Him, He will forsake you." (2 Chronicles 15:1-2). Up to this point in his life, Asa had walked with God, and for a time he continued to do so. However, later he turned from following the Lord and even imprisoned a prophet who rebuked him. He did not pay attention to the earlier warning that he could possibly forsake the Lord, and as a result, the finish to his life was marred. If God warns us of a potential weakness, we need to pay attention.

(4) It is God who gives wisdom. No matter how hard we might study, we still need God to grant wisdom to us. In fact, many learned, intelligent people have been very unwise. Wisdom is a gift from God, and the Bible encourages us to ask Him for it (James 1:5). Our study and our knowledge can certainly help us, but wisdom is the correct application of knowledge, and that is something that He grants to those who are humble and faithful.

If we have desired wisdom, and if the Lord has given us promises, we have been blessed already. Now we need to pay heed to the warnings that God gave to Solomon and walk in His ways. By so doing, we will grow in the blessings that He has given to us, in wisdom, knowledge, and understanding, and enter further into His precious promises.

TWO

PROMISES

In the previous chapter, we saw that when God appeared to Solomon, on both occasions He gave promises to him. We might ask, why would God do this? Does He give promises today?

Promises are something that direct our attention to the future, but not in a vague sense. Rather, they create an expectation within us of some specific event, or something that God will do in our lives. We can see an example of how promises impact us by looking at an employment situation. When a person is employed by a business, the employer promises to pay that employee at a certain pay rate per hour and at certain intervals, such as weekly. When the employee goes to work, the promise that the employer made to him/her has established an expectation of being paid for the work performed at the agreed rate and interval. If the employee has worked overtime, there is an expectation of a higher paycheck as compensation for the additional hours worked. The promise created an expectation and focused the employee to perform the necessary work.

The promises of God can benefit us in similar fashion. Suppose God gives us a promise of a certain quality, perhaps wisdom like He promised to Solomon. Because we have received this promise, the desire to be wise should become important to us. We should begin to take note of passages in the Bible that refer to wisdom, begin to see examples of it, and examples where there was a lack of wisdom too, so that we can learn. Our attention becomes particularly focused on wisdom, and the desire that God will establish this quality grows within us.

Another example might be a promise pertaining to the salvation of a friend or relative who is dear to us. Perhaps this person is far from God, living a life that is very contrary to the ways of God. However, the promise creates faith in us, and we pray with a believing heart because of the promise from God, not being deflected by what we see with our natural eyes, but instead seeing the outcome of the promise with our spiritual eyes.

Let us look at some promises that were given to people in the Bible. Joseph provides us with an excellent example of promises and how they came to fruition. His life is detailed in Genesis chapters 37-50. As a teenager, God gave him a dream in which he and his brothers were binding sheaves. Joseph's sheaf stood upright while the sheaves of his brothers bowed down to his sheaf. The implication was clear – Joseph would reign over his brothers. In the culture of that day, the preeminence was with the oldest son, but Joseph was the eleventh of twelve sons. Normally speaking, the likelihood of the dream being fulfilled was remote at best. Understandably, because of the culture, the older brothers did not take kindly to this dream.

Actually, that is a gross understatement. They viewed him as father's favorite, which he was, and for him to say that they would be subservient to him was outrageous. To make matters worse, Joseph had another dream in which the sun, moon, and eleven stars bowed down to him, indicating that his parents and all of his brothers would be subject to him. Such a thing was unheard of in those days, and the older brothers hated him for it.

The promises that God gave to Joseph came about in the most remarkable way. The plan of God was for Joseph to rule over Egypt, and become, in a sense, the savior of the world, including the savior of his own family. However, there were three major obstacles to the promises of God being fulfilled, in addition to a necessary work within Joseph's own heart to enable him to hold such a high office as a man of God. As we look at how God accomplished the impossible, we must understand that His ways are not our ways. God looks beyond the present circumstances at the end goal, whereas we see only the present circumstances. Consequently, we have difficulty understanding whatever is happening to us. It is so important that we hold fast in these times because God will bring us through in due course. Here are the three obstacles:

> (1) God had to get Joseph to Egypt. Joseph was living in Canaan, and he was his father's favorite son. There was no way that he was going to relocate. The thought would never have entered his head, much less that of his father who would need to approve such a move. So, God used the hatred

of his older brothers as a means to get him there. They sold him to a band of Midianites who were traveling to Egypt, where they would in turn sell Joseph as a slave, making some money from this cruel transaction.

The brothers thought that they were ridding themselves of this upstart younger brother, and now it would be impossible for him to reign over them. Joseph would be away from the family, even out of the country, so the dreams could never come to pass. Or so they thought. He was going to be a slave in a distant land for the rest of his life. But it was all in the plan of God.

(2) Having moved Joseph to Egypt, God now had to have Pharaoh meet Joseph. This was another significant hurdle because Joseph was just an unknown slave, not even an Egyptian. So how could God bring this about? The first step was to have Joseph bought by a high-ranking officer, the captain of Pharaoh's guard. This might have looked like a promising beginning for Joseph, but when the captain's wife falsely accused him of attempted rape, he put Joseph into prison.

Most of us would view this as an unlikely path to fulfilling the promises. In fact, most of us would view this as the kiss of death! Joseph was now in a secure prison where the only person in the entire world who cared about him, his father, was miles away and believed that he was dead. He may never get out, and even if he does, his reputation is ruined. Naturally speaking, his best hope in life is now to become a slave for someone else.

However, because of the captain's rank, Joseph was in Pharaoh's prison, where he came to meet Pharaoh's butler and baker, who had displeased their master and been imprisoned. This would be the path to bring Joseph and Pharaoh together.

Joseph not only had to meet Pharaoh, but he had to make such a strong, favorable impression that Pharaoh would elevate him to a pre-eminent position in the kingdom. Could this possibly happen to a foreign slave? Joseph now had two contacts with Pharaoh, but they were both in prison with him. Furthermore, they were not advisors to Pharaoh so they would not be able to speak on Joseph's behalf even if they were released. The chances of God's promises being fulfilled were still bleak.

Then one night, the butler and the baker both had dreams which Joseph correctly interpreted. He asked the butler to put in a good word for him when Pharaoh restored him to his job so that he could be released from prison. This would still not get him before Pharaoh, but at least he would be out of prison.

However, the butler forgot about Joseph and two more years passed. It is likely that the butler was not willing to risk his own future over a Hebrew slave, particularly having already done

one stint in prison for displeasing Pharaoh. So, he made no mention of Joseph. Then Pharaoh himself had dreams that greatly troubled him. Now the butler had an opportunity to make a good impression on his boss. He remembered Joseph, and how Joseph had correctly interpreted his own dream, and that of the baker too, and recommended that Pharaoh call for Joseph. Joseph interpreted Pharaoh's dreams and gave such wise advice as to how to prepare for the coming famine. Pharaoh was so impressed that he appointed Joseph to manage the country, second only to himself. It was a very complicated procedure for God to get Joseph to this point, but then how else would a foreign slave meet possibly the most powerful man in the world? It is astonishing that it ever happened. And now, Joseph is running the country. How amazing is that!

(3) The third major obstacle was for Joseph's family to travel to Egypt where they would find that he was the ruler and be subject to him. To do so, God brought a severe famine that affected not only Egypt but other lands, including Canaan where Joseph's family lived. The only place that had a food supply was Egypt, where Joseph's skillful management in the abundant years had reserved grain for the years of famine. The need for food brought firstly the older brothers to Egypt, and later the entire family. The brothers did indeed bow down to Joseph, not recognizing

him, and instead knowing him only as a powerful ruler.

The story of Joseph illustrates clearly how God is able to bring His promises to fruition, even the most unlikely ones. For the dreams that He gave to Joseph to be fulfilled, three highly improbable changes in events had to come about. There was no way that Joseph could have manipulated the circumstances himself, or even have imagined that becoming the ruler of Egypt would be part of God's plan.

We said earlier that not only were there three major obstacles to the dreams being fulfilled, but also there had to be a work of grace done in Joseph's heart:

- Joseph had to become a mature and wise man of God. For his brothers to hate him so much, he must have been unwise in the way he conducted himself, perhaps taking advantage of the fact that he was the favorite son. Also, he may have been somewhat cocky in the manner in which he told his dreams to his brothers. We would say today that Joseph needed to become a mature Christian with sound character, and growing in wisdom was part of that maturity.

- Joseph had to be able to believe God in spite of his predicaments, a belief that was grounded in the knowledge of the very nature of God. Not only did his own character have to be refined, but he had to come to really know His God. In so doing, he would be sure that God was fully able to keep His promises, no matter how impossible the circumstances might appear.

- Joseph had to come through these terrible trials without becoming bitter. If we are to grow in God, we will face trials. People will say untrue and unkind things about us, they will defraud us, betray us, and take advantage of us. It is during trials that the things we believe are proven. Do we really believe that God is faithful? That is still just a theory to us until we have been in a situation where it is essential for us that God be faithful.

  As we pass through these trials, we develop confidence in His character, and the theory becomes fact and knowledge. Sometimes in a trial, it seems as if God has let us down, and in these times we are faced with a decision…will we believe Him or not? What do we really think about God and His character? If we continue to trust Him through the darkest of times, we ultimately find that He is indeed faithful and our relationship with Him grows.

  Joseph's brothers had done a terrible thing to him, their own brother. They had even lied to their father to cover up their deed. In Egypt, as ruler of the country, Joseph was in a position to take revenge, which he did not. His understanding of the hand of God in his life and his forgiveness of the brothers was apparent in his behavior toward them.

Not fully understanding this, after Jacob their father had died, the brothers were fearful of revenge and told Joseph that they were his servants in hopes of preserving their lives. However, Joseph said to them, "Do not be afraid, for am I in the place of God? But as for you, you meant evil against me, but God meant it for good, in order to bring it about as it is this day, to save many people alive. Now therefore, do not be afraid. I will provide for you, and your little ones." (Genesis 50:19-21). Joseph had come through his trials with an understanding of the ways of God, and with impeccable character.

In Psalm 105, the psalmist provides us with additional information regarding things that happened to Joseph in his trials. We read of the painful experiences that he suffered in prison. Then the psalmist makes an unusual statement in verse 19 where we read, "Until his word came to pass, the word of the Lord tried him." This sounds confusing at first, but it reveals a crucial aspect to our maturing spiritually and coming to truly know God.

Joseph had been given a word from God, promises in his dreams. However, his life had taken such a catastrophic turn that all hope of the fulfillment seemed lost. The very promises became a point of testing. Could God do the impossible? Was His promise any good? And to make this personal, what do you and I really think about His power and His nature? Until the time comes for God to bring His promise into reality, the promise itself becomes an instrument for testing us and purifying us.

In 1972, my wife's parents went to the Olympic Games in Munich, Germany, as adult leaders of a youth outreach. They were living in New Zealand at the time, and while in Munich the Lord said that He would bring them back to that country. The reason was not obvious, nor was the means. Although respected in church circles in their own country, they were unknown elsewhere.

About fifteen years later, they had moved to the Seattle area and met an Englishman who invited my father-in-law to minister at a conference in England. While at the conference, he met a German man who invited him to Germany. This began an extremely fruitful ministry, primarily in Germany and Switzerland. They traveled to Europe one-to-two times each year, each visit lasting about two months, ministering to many people. These visits continued for the next twenty-five years. God had given them a promise, and in His timetable He engineered the circumstances to bring it to pass.

I would like to illustrate the importance of holding fast during times of trial, and how in time, God will bring us through into a closer relationship with Himself. For about ten years, my wife had suffered serious medical issues that mystified doctors and caused her considerable physical hardship and stress. One day, she had a vision. She entered a tunnel at the base of a mountain. The tunnel was very dark so that she could not see where she was going, and had to feel the walls to avoid walking into them. The experience depicted what she had endured for the past ten years, a time of darkness, not knowing where it was leading or how she could get out of it.

Presently, there was a light ahead. She continued walking toward the light and soon emerged from the tunnel on the side of the mountain. To her surprise, she could see the entrance to the tunnel which was well below her. While in the tunnel, she had been climbing without realizing it. This climbing represented growth in her spiritual life. Then the Lord spoke to her and said that from now on, she would climb on the face of the mountain and not in a tunnel. In the subsequent fifteen years, she has continued to have difficulties such as one would expect when climbing a mountain, but never since has she been in a dark tunnel. The vision and the promise were a great encouragement to us both, and God has kept His promise.

If we are to mature in our Christian walk, our beliefs have to be tried. Our knowledge of God cannot be theoretical, Someone we only know about. God has to become Someone who we know, in ever-increasing measure. We want to become people who can place our full trust in God because we have come to truly know Him.

THREE

GOD'S PERSPECTIVE

In the previous chapter, we discussed how God had given a promise to Joseph through dreams, and how, against all odds, the promise came to fulfillment. Let us now look a little closer at the events from God's perspective, rather than from Joseph's. I do say this with reservation because I cannot claim to be able to speak for God, but with the benefit of hindsight, we can see aspects of His plan and purpose.

It is important for us to remember that God knows the end of a matter even before the events begin to unfold (Isaiah 46:10). It is also important to remember that He is always in control of circumstances (Isaiah 55:11). Sometimes it may appear to the contrary, but God has never surrendered His sovereignty, and He never will (Romans 8:28). The powers of evil may seem to triumph in the short term, but never in the long term.

We see this with Joseph. God's plan actually extended back in time to his great-grandfather, Abraham. God had promised Abraham that his descendants would inherit the land of Canaan, and that they would be a great nation of many people. God also said that Abraham's descendants would live in a foreign land for a time, that they would leave that land in the fourth generation with great possessions, and return to Canaan to occupy it as their own land. (Genesis 13:14-17, 15:14-17). All these amazing promises were made before Abraham had even a single descendant!

God is certainly not afraid to make promises because He knows that He can fulfill them. In fact, that is something that distinguishes the Bible from all other books…it is full of promises (or prophecies), most of which have been fulfilled and can be verified by history. The ones that have not been fulfilled relate to future events so their verification is yet to come.

The promises that God made to Abraham, He confirmed to Abraham's son, Isaac, and to Abraham's grandson, Jacob, who was the father of Joseph. By the time Jacob moved to Egypt, the family consisted of only seventy people, not exactly a nation. However, when they came out of Egypt under the leadership of Moses, they had become a great nation in only four generations (Moses' great grandfather was Levi, one of the sons of Jacob who relocated to Egypt, and the first of the four generations). Moses took a census of the people thirteen months after they left Egypt, and we are told that there were 653,550 men who were able to go to war (Numbers 1:45-46). This census excluded the tribe of Levi, women, children under twenty, and the elderly. If we assume that those able to go to war were aged between twenty and fifty, we can speculate that the total population was at least 2.5 million.

GOD'S PERSPECTIVE

We know that a Pharaoh who came to power sometime after the death of Joseph was fearful of the population growth of Israel, so he made them slaves in order to control them (Exodus 1:8-11). We might ask ourselves two questions:

(1) What would have transpired if Israel had remained in Canaan and not relocated to Egypt?

It is very possible that Jacob and his family would have died in the famine, but assuming they survived, the surrounding nations would have viewed their expanding population as a threat, just as Pharaoh did. It is most likely that those nations would have banded together and killed the Israelites, wiping them out completely or at least diminishing their numbers so that the threat was removed.

(2) What would have happened had Pharaoh not made them slaves?

Without that hardship, it is very likely that the people would have been content to remain in Egypt. The land of Goshen where they dwelt was suitable for their livestock, and to move the whole nation back to Canaan was a major undertaking. Something drastic had to happen to make them want to leave Egypt.

We can see then, that to preserve the descendants of Abraham, it was necessary for them to grow in a safe place outside the Promised Land, and that they would then need a significant incentive to relocate back to that land. As we noted above, God was looking at the end of the matter. His plan was not going to be thwarted by anything. He would shield Jacob and his family in Egypt where they could grow into a large nation, able to drive out the inhabitants of Canaan and possess it, and allow them to be so harshly oppressed that they would want to leave Egypt.

The brothers sold Joseph to the Midianites out of their hatred for him, but in Psalm 105:17, we read God's perspective on it. We read that He "...sent a man before them – Joseph..." We can be very sure that neither Joseph nor his brothers viewed the sale of Joseph into slavery to be a step in the plan of God, at least not at that time. However, to God, looking forward to the end of the matter, this was a part of the plan to fulfill His promise to Abraham.

Having relocated Joseph, God then had to prepare him for the great task of leading the nation in trying times. Joseph would need to be a skilled manager of people and of resources. He would also need to be a strong leader. When Joseph was purchased by Potiphar, he became a trusted servant because the Lord was with him and everything he did prospered. We read that Potiphar "...left all that he had in Joseph's hand, and he did not know what he had except for the bread which he ate." (Genesis 39:6). This was a position of absolute trust. In it, Joseph would learn management of a considerable estate (for Potiphar would have been wealthy), and also he had to exercise perfect character in order to maintain that trust.

However, Joseph must have needed further training. This came about when Potiphar's wife falsely accused him of attempted rape, simply out of spite, and his master committed him to Pharaoh's prison. Once again, he rose to a position of trust. The keeper of the prison put him in charge and "...

did not look into anything that was under Joseph's authority because the Lord was with him: and whatever he did, the Lord made it prosper." (Genesis 39:23).

By the time that he was released from prison, Joseph had gained about twelve years of management experience. Moreover, and more importantly, his character was purified, as shown by the fact that he was fully trusted in everything that was under him. Both Potiphar and the jailer recognized his worth. Also, Joseph was learning how to lead people, even difficult people. Slaves would tend to try to get out of their duties, and prisoners were in the prison because of character deficiencies. Joseph had to lead them in a manner that they respected or he would not have been successful.

There were two more important character issues that could qualify or disqualify Joseph for God's service. Firstly, he had to forgive those who betrayed him; his brothers and Potiphar's wife, and even the butler who forgot about him for two long years. Had Joseph not passed this test, he might have been vengeful toward his brothers, which would have been detrimental to God's plan to preserve the family and protect them in Egypt. And secondly, he had to believe God.

When the Bible says that God is faithful, is that something that we really know? Is it still true when something in our life goes very wrong? Joseph had to come to such a knowledge of God that he could believe for the impossible. He must have faith in God, regardless of the circumstances. This level of faith and trust cannot be manufactured or an act that we perform. It has to be something that we know. The true, unfailing, loving, merciful, kind, nature of God has to be a reality in our lives. And it only comes about as a result of passing through trials.

Sometimes, we have to wait for God to move. Not knowing how long the waiting period will be makes this difficult. If we knew that God's promise would come about in say, two years, we would be able to hang in there and see it through. However, what often happens is that there is no evidence of God moving until one day, everything changes suddenly and dramatically. When God moves, it is often rapid and decisive. The difficulty for us is that while God knows the end from the beginning, we see only the middle and the circumstances that we are experiencing. This is why we must grow in our relationship with the Lord, so that we know Him and can have confidence in Him.

We have discussed these principles from the life of Joseph because the Bible narrative provides us with much detail regarding his life. Let us now return to Solomon. We noted that God had given him some wonderful promises. Solomon would have wisdom and knowledge that surpassed all others. God truly fulfilled this promise, and the kings of the earth sought him out to learn from him. God also promised him wealth, and without any doubt, Solomon and his kingdom became exceedingly wealthy. Part of his wealth came from the gifts that he received from other kings, but much of it was due to his having a good business sense, which is something that God must have granted him as a means to fulfill the promise.

We saw how Joseph was a man of superb character, which was important, probably essential, to his fully receiving his promises. Unfortunately, the same was not true for Solomon. He started well, but later in life, allowed his foreign wives to turn him from wholeheartedly following the Lord. As a result, the promise of long life was denied him because he did not walk in the ways of David. Perhaps Solomon had a weakness whereby he wanted to please his wives. Perhaps his interests

GOD'S PERSPECTIVE

began to supplant his zeal for the Lord, much like in the Parable of the Sower where the good seed was "choked with cares, riches, and pleasures of life…" (Luke 8:14). Perhaps it was something else, but certainly, it resulted in a failing after having accomplished so much good in the earlier years of his life.

Whatever the reason, there was an area in Solomon's life that he never dealt with. It resulted in his not receiving a promise, and brought devastating consequences to the kingdom, which was divided after his death. His life provides a sober warning to us not to accommodate an area of weakness, but to earnestly seek the Lord for His victory over it.

There is one more aspect to our promises being fulfilled, and this may well be the most important. Although the promises are given to us, the fulfillment is for the glory of God. If we fail to understand this, our promises might be delayed or even fail. In the case of many promises, the fulfillment is not so that we can be elevated, but for Him to be glorified through us.

The prophet Daniel understood this. He began to pray earnestly for God to move and fulfill His promise to return the people to their homeland. Jeremiah had prophesied that after seventy years of captivity in Babylon, the Jews would return to Judea and now the seventy years had passed. Daniel's prayer is recorded in Daniel chapter nine. It is a humble prayer, petitioning God on the basis of His mercy and not because a return to Judea and Jerusalem is in any way deserved. In verse nineteen, we read the cry of Daniel's heart. "Oh Lord, hear! Oh Lord, forgive! Oh Lord, listen and act! Do not delay for Your own sake, my God, for Your city and Your people who are called by Your name." Notice the reasons that Daniel gives for God to act. It is for His sake, not the people's. And also, it is because God's reputation is tied to His people and the city of Jerusalem.

Daniel did not tell God that He had to release the people because He had promised to do so. Rather, Daniel's reasoning was that God should do this for the sake of His own name. God's reputation among the nations was inescapably linked to Jerusalem and the Jews, and Daniel was mindful of this. Daniel understood that the release of the people from captivity was necessary because God had promised it. However, although the people would benefit from the release, it would be enacted so that God would be glorified through it. The glory of God, and not of us, is an essential ingredient to the fulfillment of many of His promises.

FOUR

SOLOMON'S WEALTH

Solomon was a wealthy man. Really wealthy. His wealth is well documented in the Bible, and we read that in his day, gold was so plentiful that silver was regarded as being of little value. (1 Kings 10:21). There must have an abundance of silver in the kingdom, however, because it was "...as common in Jerusalem as stones..." (1 Kings 10:27). Silver was still useful to Solomon, however, because he could use it for trading with other nations who were not as wealthy as Israel (1 Kings 10:29).

We have some statistics related to the gold that Solomon received, which gives us insight to the extent of his wealth. On one trading venture to Ophir, Solomon's men brought back 420 talents of gold (1 Kings 9:28). A talent is the equivalent of about 75 pounds, and the current value of a pound of gold is approximately $18,400. Therefore, in today's values, this single venture brought Solomon $580 million dollars.

We also read that Solomon received 666 talents of gold each year (1 Kings 10:14). We don't know for how many years this continued, but a single year was worth more than $900 million dollars in today's money. The Bible tells us that this does not take into consideration the gold that came from merchants, traders, and kings of other regions. The bottom line…Solomon was worth a bundle! He was probably the richest man in all of history.

Most of us would like to be rich, or at least have sufficient wealth that we could be insulated from financial pressures and economic downturns. Almost all of us experience financial struggles at some point in life, and long to be in a position where we feel financially secure. I do believe that these struggles are important for our spiritual growth, as our attitude toward money can reveal things about our heart. Solomon understood this. In Ecclesiastes 7:14, he wrote that we should rejoice in times of prosperity, but in times of adversity, we should realize that God gives both. In other words, we need to be thankful to God for His provision, not neglecting to remember that it is He who enables us to have income. The adverse times are uncomfortable, but these are the times when we grow spiritually.

Of course, what one person considers wealth may not be the same for another. More importantly than trying to define wealth, we must realize that with money comes considerable responsibility. Let us for a moment consider a hypothetical situation where a wealthy, generous person hears of a church that needs one million dollars to enlarge their sanctuary. The person believes this to be a church that is sound in doctrine and purpose, and is confident that a gift would be made to a good cause. What should the person do? By giving the money, the church is enabled to go forward, which is good. However, what if God wanted to provide that money through many smaller donations, thereby stretching the congregation and enabling them to grow spiritually. The wealthy person who gave the million dollars could be the Lord's source of provision, or he/she could be an obstacle to His plan because the opportunity for the people to grow in faith has been denied. A person who has money carries a great responsibility to walk closely with the Lord because they can be a solution or an obstacle.

The requirement for a wealthy person to walk uprightly in the fear of the Lord is very high indeed. They must hear what God is saying so that they give when the time is right and withhold when God has a different plan. The same principle applies to those who are not wealthy, but face similar situations of a lesser magnitude. There is a requirement to be generous, but that is a requirement of all of us. We are to be generous, based on our capabilities.

The Bible is very commending of generous people. There is, however, an important principle that is often related to giving, namely, that obedience is what really counts with God. To illustrate, the Lord had instructed King Saul to go to battle with the Amalekites and to destroy them because of their wickedness. In fact, Israel was not even to keep the livestock as spoil from the victory (1 Samuel 15:1-3). Although God is very merciful, it seems that there comes a time when the extent of wickedness in a people reaches a point where there is no return, as evidenced by the Flood in the days of Noah, and Judah before the Babylonian invasion. This must have been the case with the Amalekites. So what did Saul do? He defeated the Amalekites but spared their king and the best of the livestock.

Later, when the prophet Samuel confronted him, Saul said that he had obeyed the word of the Lord but the people had kept the livestock to sacrifice to the Lord (1 Samuel 15:15, 20-21). Saul attempted to shift the blame from himself, but in verse nine we read that Saul was just as involved in sparing the livestock as were the people.

Saul's response to Samuel sounds very spiritual. He said that he had kept the best of the livestock for the purpose of offering sacrifices to the Lord. What could be better than that, to honor the Lord with the very best! But Samuel replied, "…to obey is better than sacrifice…" (1 Samuel 15:22).

Sometimes, the Lord will ask something of us that we do not want to do, and we refuse. Perhaps our refusal is not as blatant as was Jonah's, when he boarded a ship for Tarshish, sailing in the opposite direction from Nineveh, the place that God had called him to go to and preach. Usually our disobedience is more subtle, sometimes even cloaked with a spiritual-sounding reason like King Saul, but then our conscience troubles us and we feel that we have to make up for our disobedience. Instead of being obedient, we begin to make sacrifices, and a very common sacrifice that people turn to is the giving of money.

As an example, perhaps the Lord called us to a missionary venture, but we were not obedient and remained at home. In order to alleviate our conscience, we do the next best thing…we donate to the mission. The fact that we donate is a good thing, but it is not what the Lord actually asked of us. Obedience is better than sacrifice, and disobedience cannot be compensated by some sacrificial act.

Another important principle regarding money relates to attention seeking. As a practical matter, seldom can our giving be completely confidential, but we are not to seek attention and publicize it. Jesus described it as not letting our left hand know what our right hand is doing (Matthew 6:3). Furthermore, He was critical of the Pharisees, who we are told, were lovers of money and lovers of the praise of the people. Money can be such a blessing, and also such a problem. Jesus understood this perfectly, saying that it all depends on what is in our hearts. (Luke 16:14-15).

Whether we are wealthy or not, it is important that we have a generous heart. Certainly, God is very generous to us and we need to grow in His nature. Proverbs 11:24 says, "There is one who scatters, yet increases more; and there is one that withholds more than is right, but it leads to poverty." In this proverb, there are three important principles for us to understand.

- Firstly, the person who scattered (gave of what they had), increased their wealth. Although they gave away, God saw to it that not only were they replenished, but they actually had more. However, let us not think that the path to increasing our wealth is to give away what we have so that God will give back to us double or some other multiple. God will not be manipulated, and such an attitude reveals a heart that needs correction, because the emphasis is on increasing one's wealth instead of being obedient to God.

- Secondly, the person who withheld ended with less. One would have expected the opposite, that by keeping one's money, one would at least remain at the same financial level. However, God blesses people with a generous heart.

- Thirdly, of the person who withheld, it says that they withheld more than what was right. This tells us that our giving has to be conducted prayerfully, because the money that we have needs to be used wisely. If we give away more than we should, we will not have sufficient for our needs and those of our family. God has provided for those needs, usually through our jobs, and it is correct for us to retain a portion of our income to cover them. It is not right for us to give away funds that God has provided to be allocated to certain needs, such as food and clothing. One other point…giving away our money could be affected by our spending too much on the wrong things. If we do not handle money wisely we will not have sufficient.

We should note that frequently, the return on our generosity is not measured in material things. It may be in more important things, such as a closer relationship with God, greater peace in our lives, or some other blessing. These are eternal and therefore of more value than finances. That said, I do believe that if we are wise, prayerful, and obedient with our finances, God will take care of our material needs.

While we are talking about money, we should make some comments regarding tithing. Some consider it to be a concept that was in the Law, and that because we are under grace through Jesus, it no longer has application to our lives. However, let us consider the first occasion when tithing is mentioned in the Bible. One of the principles of hermeneutics is that we should examine the initial introduction of a spiritual doctrine, because it will contain the seed for the entire doctrine. The first account of tithing is recorded in Genesis 14:18-20 where Abraham gave a tithe of his spoils to Melchizedek.

This event took place long before the Law was given on Mount Sinai, so although tithing was included in the Law, it did not originate with the law. Here we have none other than Abraham, the very Father of Faith, giving a tithe to a man who is a type of the Lord Jesus.

In Romans chapter four, Paul makes it very clear that Abraham's righteousness predated the giving of the Law. His righteousness was through faith, which we are to follow. Likewise, his tithing predates the Law, thereby establishing it as a principle for us too. Psalm 110:4 tells us that Jesus is a "Priest forever after the order of Melchizedek", and this is quoted in Hebrews 5:6 as part of the explanation for Christ being the High Priest for a New Covenant. Melchizedek was both a priest and a king, a joint role that could not be held by a single person under the Law, but is the role of Christ. We can see then, from this first occurrence, that tithing is a principle that we need to follow and is unrelated to the Law.

We should also examine the attitude of Jesus pertaining to tithing. In Matthew 23:23, Jesus is reprimanding the Pharisees for being so precise over the small matter of paying a tithe on herbs in order to keep the Law, when they neglected the more important matters of justice, mercy, and faith. He then goes on to say, "These you ought to have done, without leaving the others undone." In other words, while Jesus was appalled at how the Pharisees overlooked important matters of the Law, He did approve of the fact that they tithed by saying, "These you ought to have done..."

From these passages of the Bible, we can make the following statements regarding tithing:

- Tithing predates the Law.

- It was introduced by the Father of Faith (Abraham), not the father of the Law (Moses).

- Abraham tithed to no lesser a person than Melchizedek who was the Biblical type of Christ as the priest of the New Covenant.

- Tithing was endorsed by Jesus during His earthly ministry.

- We can therefore conclude that tithing is applicable to modern-day Christians.

To summarize, one final word regarding our use of money – it carries responsibility, whether we have a lot or a little.

FIVE

SOLOMON'S WISDOM

Of all the qualities and acts of Solomon, the one that he is best known for is his wisdom. Truly, he was an exceptionally wise man, although he also made some very unwise decisions.

His wisdom began as a young king. Solomon had inherited the kingdom of his father David, and God appeared to him in a dream soon afterward, offering to grant a request that he could choose to make. We could liken this to Psalm 37:4, "Delight yourself in the Lord and He will give you the desires of your heart." It is clear that God loved Solomon. He appeared to him twice, and called him "Jedidiah" which means "friend of God." It is quite a privilege for God to grant us a new name, especially one with such a wonderful meaning.

When Solomon asked for wisdom to govern the people, God was immensely pleased with his response and granted his request to the extent that the wisdom that He gave to Solomon exceeded all others who had lived before him, and those who would live after him, except, of course, for the Lord Jesus (1 Kings 3:12). Solomon was able to teach on a wide variety of subjects including not just spiritual things but all manner of animals, fish, birds, and vegetation. The men of all nations came to learn from him.

Very soon after he came to the throne, the wisdom that God had given to Solomon was evident to all. In 1 Kings 3:16-28, we have the account of two women who lived together and both gave birth to sons only a few days apart. Both women slept with their children in their own bed. One woman's child died during the night, and while the other woman was asleep, she exchanged children. In the morning, the other woman recognized that the living child was hers, but the first woman maintained that it was her child. The matter came to Solomon for his ruling. Today, we could conduct DNA testing to establish the identity of the true mother, but nothing like that was available to Solomon. Instead, he called for a sword and declared that because there was no way to determine who the real mother was, the living child would be cut in two and each woman receive one half. This caused the true mother to seek to protect her child by offering him to the other woman. Solomon knew that a true mother would protect her child, even at her own expense, and by his threat of death, the truth was revealed.

When we consider that at this time, Solomon was only nineteen or twenty years of age, his actions to determine the true mother showed astounding wisdom. He correctly judged that when the life of the child was at stake, the true mother would be more concerned with her child's safety than her own fulfillment. Very few people of his age, particularly men, would understand the strength of a mother's heart for her child. But Solomon did because God had given great wisdom to him.

How can we define wisdom? One definition in a dictionary says, "A soundness of action or decision with regard to the application of experience, knowledge, and good judgement." More simply put, wisdom is correctly applying knowledge to a given situation. Wisdom enables us to make sound decisions, just as Solomon did with the two women and their children.

We can learn some lessons about wisdom from God's workings in the life of Solomon. One lesson is that when Solomon asked for wisdom, it showed that he valued things that God valued. He did not ask for riches, long life, or a successful reign. Instead, he showed humility, recognizing that if he was to govern God's people well, as his father had done, he was going to need the quality of wisdom. Solomon valued character above fame and fortune. As we read the Bible, it is very clear that God does too. In fact, Proverbs 4:7 tells us that wisdom is the principal thing. Proverbs 8:11 says that anything else we can desire cannot be compared to wisdom. These are strong statements indeed and clearly indicate that God views wisdom as the most valuable quality that we can possess.

Another lesson for us is that wisdom is a gift from God. Solomon did not obtain his wisdom from much study, although that can definitely help. Our study increases our knowledge, providing us with more information that can be correctly applied in a given situation. However, study and our own efforts will not make us wise. No, wisdom was something that

God gave to Solomon, not something that he generated by his own efforts. Proverbs 2:6 states this fact clearly, telling us that, "The Lord gives wisdom." This is confirmed in James 1:5, where the apostle writes that if we lack wisdom, we can ask God and He will give it to us. Wisdom is a gift from God, and He alone is truly wise. Often when we look at how He has handled a situation, we have to acknowledge that His way was the right way and our solution would not have had the same lasting impact. I have seen this on many occasions.

Another lesson for us from Solomon's life is that while wisdom should keep us from making bad decisions, that is not necessarily the case. The desires of our own heart can overrule the best course that we should take. Solomon, for all of his wisdom, made some very unwise decisions, and they set the stage for the division of the kingdom after his death, early in the reign of his son, Rehoboam. It is really quite astounding that this man, the wisest of all time other than Jesus, could make such poor decisions. No wonder that the Bible exhorts us, "Keep your heart with all diligence for out of it spring the issues of life." (Proverbs 4:23).

We have seen that Solomon initially valued the things that God valued. However, he violated the clear command of God regarding wives. God had said, that a king should not, "... multiply wives for himself, lest his heart turn away." Solomon had seven hundred wives and three hundred concubines (1 Kings 11:3), and the result was just as God had warned, his heart was turned away. It was customary in those days for a king to give his daughter as the wife for another king as part of a treaty between the two men and their nations. Consequently, Solomon had wives from many different nations because all the nations wanted to have a good relationship with him. Indeed his first wife was the daughter of Pharaoh, king of Egypt, and it seems that she held a special place in his heart.

Solomon's wives brought with them the religious practices of their homelands, which centered on the worship of foreign gods. In time, Solomon followed his wives in the worship of these gods, greatly displeasing the Lord. Like having many wives, worshiping gods other than the one true God is also a violation of a clear command from God. The prohibition is found in many passages of the Bible, including the Ten Commandments, where we read, "You shall have no other gods before Me." (Exodus 20:3)

In this, we see how an exceedingly wise man made an exceedingly unwise decision. A requirement of kings was to write out a copy of the Law for themselves (Deuteronomy 17:18), so Solomon knew the unmistakable command from God not to have many wives, and also the unmistakable command not to engage in the practices of worshiping foreign gods. Yet Solomon followed the dictates of his heart. Consequently, his wisdom did not protect him as it should have. When we break God's commands, we will suffer the consequences and reap what we have sown, as did Solomon, and unfortunately, the whole nation. Leaders have a particular responsibility to be true to God's commands, as usually those under them are blessed or suffer as a result of the leaders' decisions.

A point that we should note regarding Solomon's excessive number of wives and concubines is that this was an hereditary issue. His father, David, had seventeen wives, which pales by comparison compared to Solomon, but nevertheless is a substantial number. Further, David committed adultery with

Bathsheba. This spiritual problem associated with women was passed on to his son. Sometimes we have to break spiritual bondages in our lives that are hereditary in nature in order to progress in our walk with God.

The lesson of Solomon's disobedience presents a lesson for us regarding the importance of keeping God's commands. These commands have been given to us for our own good. If we happen to not like a certain command, we should still obey it, because otherwise we will reap the harvest of what we have sown. If we sowed in disobedience, we cannot expect to reap blessing. Blessing is the harvest that grows from the seeds of obedience.

As a young man, I had been talking to a couple who were living together while engaged. They justified living together before marriage on the grounds that they loved each other and would soon be married. Neither of them had the slightest intention of pursuing another relationship. They were being faithful to each other and would continue to be faithful throughout their marriage.

Now the command of God is that we abstain from intimate relations until we are married, and then remain faithful thereafter. This couple intended to keep the second part of that command but justified their breaking of the first. What they were saying had some logic to it, and I really did not know how to answer them. I asked the Lord to help me understand why such a couple should not "jump the gun." Why would it matter, so long as they did in fact marry and live true to each other for the rest of their lives? His reply was very simple. He said, "Because I asked them not to."

If we break God's commands, it is possible that we may appear to be unaffected, but typically, if we are loose in one area of our life we will be loose in other areas too, and somewhere, we will pay a price for our disobedience. How the Lord answered me is very telling. If He asks us not to do something and we reject it, what does that say about our relationship with Him? Can we honestly say that we love Him? Is it possible to truly call Him our Lord, and to worship Him as such while ignoring what He says? Jesus said that we demonstrate our love for Him by keeping His commands (John 14:21). All of them. Not just the ones that suit us.

I have observed that people who are disobedient plateau in their walk with God. We might be nice people, consistent in church attendance. However, unless we deal with that issue of disobedience, confessing it and sincerely apologizing to the Lord, we just don't grow, or at least not noticeably. God reveals His ways to those who love Him, and our love is demonstrated by our obedience.

Another lesson in wisdom that we can learn from Solomon has to do with favoritism, and again we see a very unwise decision that had long-term consequences. Solomon had enormous requirements for food to support his Court and his standing army. He set up twelve governors over the nation, and they were responsible for providing that food and other supplies, each for one month of the year. However, in the divisions of the land under these governors, he excluded his own tribe, Judah. It would be like the United States requiring income tax from residents of all states, except one large state like California. This would surely breed resentment among the other states, or in Solomon's case, the other districts.

To make matters worse, Solomon's governors were mostly from the tribe of Judah or pro-Judah through marriage into Solomon's family (1 Kings 4:11-16). This favoritism created resentment amongst the northern tribes. Favoritism is hard to deal with. It happens in families, and other arenas too, such as business.

I have seen people receive promotions that were undeserving, simply because in some way the person had obtained the approval of the boss. It could be because the boss enjoyed the company of that employee, perhaps with a common interest or over drinks after work. Sadly, sometimes a better qualified employee is overlooked and the business suffers, while the lesser employee holds the position and the higher paycheck. However, none of these things escape the attention of Almighty God. Should we be on the wrong end of favoritism, it is important that we hold fast to godly principles and that our character is refined through the trial. In due course, God will reward us.

It is surprising how people will choose unwisely, even when they have been given a clear example to follow. Such was the case with Rehoboam, Solomon's son and successor. He was in his forties' when he became king, so he had many years in his adult life to observe the wisdom of his father, and also his father's regret over his disobedience to God. However, when Rehoboam could have secured the kingdom under him, he instead made a decision that would alienate the northern tribes by declaring that his treatment of them would be much harsher than that of Solomon. The result was that the kingdom was divided, and he reigned over only the southern kingdom, two of the twelve tribes.

To summarize, the lessons for us regarding wisdom are:

- It is something we should value highly and seek diligently.

- It is an integral aspect of the nature of God.

- Wisdom will enable us to make right decisions, because it is the correct application of knowledge to a given situation.

- We must guard our hearts, unless a wrong desire should overrule a wise decision.

SIX

WISDOM, AND THE FEAR OF THE LORD

The Bible has much to say about wisdom, and all of it is complimentary. It is a quality that is highly prized. Here are some of the statements regarding wisdom, all from the book of Proverbs:

- Proverbs 4:7 Wisdom is the principal thing.

- Proverbs 8:11 All things one may desire cannot be compared to her.

- He who gets wisdom loves his own soul.

In these and many other passages, we are encouraged to become wise, and the more we read about wisdom, the more we see its benefits. Certainly, God is wise. If we have been a Christian for some length of time, we will be able to refer to many instances where we thought a certain direction was best, but God did something quite unexpected. We could see the wisdom behind His actions because the outcome was better than it would have been under our intentions.

If wisdom is so valuable and important to us, the question then is, how can we become wise? Fortunately for us, the Bible provides the answer.

In several places, such as Psalm 111:10, we read that, "The fear of the Lord is the beginning of wisdom." Everything we do has a beginning. If we are constructing a building, we need to prepare the site before the actual construction can begin. If we are traveling overseas, we have to first reach the airport in order to board the aircraft. Someone said that two of the hardest things in life are starting and finishing, and understanding where to begin is essential in any project.

The Bible tells us that if we want to be wise, we must have the fear of the Lord in our lives. Therefore, it is essential that we understand what the fear of the Lord actually is in order to be able to apply it. In the phrase, "fear of the Lord," there are two key words. One is "fear" and the other is "the Lord." If we take the phrase literally, this would tend to suggest that we are supposed to be afraid of the Lord. However, that concept runs contrary to how He is revealed in the Bible, and also in our experience of walking with Him. God is actually a wonderful person, loving, forgiving, generous, and kind. Here are a few examples of verses that give us insight as to His nature.

- The apostle John wrote that "God is love." (1 John 4:8).

- One of the best-known verses in all of the Bible is John 3:16, which says, "God so loved the world that He gave His only begotten son…"

- When God showed his glory to Moses, the first quality that He mentioned was merciful. The other qualities were gracious, longsuffering, abounding in goodness and in truth. (Exodus 34:6).

- The fruit of the Spirit is love, joy, peace, longsuffering, kindness, goodness, faithfulness, gentleness, and self-control (Galatians 5:22-23). These are qualities of God that are to be worked into our lives too.

The above passages from the Bible declare the nature of God, and He is certainly not someone we should be fearing in the sense of being afraid of Him. In fact, the only time we should be afraid of God is when we are being deliberately disobedient. In these circumstances, we will suffer consequences. Usually, it is not because God steps in to punish us, although there are instances of that, such as with Ananias and Sapphira (Acts chapter 5), and King Herod (Acts chapter 12). Far more common are the consequences that come from reaping what we have sown. We bring the consequences upon ourselves through our own bad decisions.

What then is meant by "the fear of the Lord?" We will understand it better if we regard it as a term, rather than a literal description. We have many terms and expressions that we use in everyday conversation that, if taken literally, would not be understood. For example, if we are exasperated by someone, such as a parent with a naughty child, we might say, "You are driving me up the wall!" Obviously, there is no driving involved and neither is there a wall to travel up. It is an expression. Another example is the expression, "That's cool!" We use this frequently to convey our approval of something, such as an achievement, an event, or even an item of clothing. Our use of the word, "cool" has nothing to do with temperature, so someone unfamiliar with the expression would have great difficulty understanding what we mean if they interpreted the words literally. To add to the difficulty of understanding what we are saying, in some instances, "cool" and "hot" can mean the same thing. The words are expressions, and the meaning that we apply cannot be understood from a literal interpretation.

Similarly, the "fear of the Lord" is not about being afraid of God, although it does involve God and there is an aspect of fear that we should consider. Let us look at two definitions, a dictionary definition and a Bible definition.

A dictionary definition is as follows – "A very deep respect, profound reverence, and awe." This conveys that our attitude toward God is not in any way casual or disrespectful, but one where we hold Him in the highest regard. In Isaiah 66:2, God describes the kind of person that He will look at. Essentially, it is someone who is humble and takes His word very seriously. To illustrate, a few years ago, I had dinner with a king. He was the King of Tonga, an island nation in the South Pacific, and I had met him in school when we were in the same class. (I grew up in New Zealand, and his parents had sent him there for his education). Some forty years later, we made contact again by email. He was soon coming to Los Angeles and invited me to meet him for dinner.

At school, we were peers. He did not receive any special treatment, and I would tackle him when playing rugby with the same force as any other opponent. However, now he was a king. I thought carefully regarding what I should wear to dinner. After all, my best jeans were not fitting attire for a king, but perhaps a suit was being overdressed because we were renewing an old friendship. (In the end, I wore slacks, a tie and sports coat. It turned out to be very similar to his attire. Phew!) I took a gift, because one should not come before a king without a gift. What sort of a gift should I bring? Something of value, but not too expensive because again, this was a friendship. (I gave him a pictorial book of my city, and a copy of a WWII book that I had published. I knew he liked WWII books, so I thought he would enjoy it).

When I arrived where he was staying, I was asked by one of his staff to sit in the living room while I waited for him. I sat on a couch, but was quickly told to move from there to a chair. Obviously, the couch was where the king liked to sit, so I moved immediately. He soon joined me and was very warm, not at all overbearing, which put me at ease. And sure enough, he sat on the couch. He asked if I would like a cup of tea. I think all British Commonwealth citizens drink tea... except me. But a king had offered me tea, so I accepted his offer and we drank tea together and talked for a while before leaving for a restaurant. I am sure that I could have prevailed on the friendship and avoided the cup of tea without offending him, but I was respectful of the fact that he was a king, not just an old friend.

We had dinner twice over a period of three months, and I truly enjoyed both occasions, as I am sure he did also. We covered various subjects, including of course, our school years and having a relationship with God. However, I was always mindful that he was no longer a peer. He was the king of a nation. This caused me to be respectful. I don't think I met the standard of "A very deep respect, profound reverence, and awe," in my attitude towards him, but certainly it was far from casual. If I would treat a fellow human being, with respect because of his office, how much more should I treat the King of Kings because of His Office? This is "fear" in the sense of "the fear of the Lord."

In the previous chapter, we discussed how Solomon determined who was the mother of the living child. The wisdom that he displayed in resolving this dilemma was remarkable, particularly when we consider his age. The account also provides us with insight regarding the use of the word, "fear." In 1 Kings 3:28 we read, "All Israel...feared the king, for they saw that the wisdom of God was in him to administer justice." Were they afraid of Solomon, perhaps fearing that he would be a violent ruler? No, they were in awe of his wisdom. The verse says that they feared him, and this is the same fear that we must have with the fear of the Lord in our life. A very deep respect, profound reverence, and awe.

Let us now consider a Bible definition, which is as follows – "The fear of the Lord is to hate evil." (Proverbs 8:13). What does the Bible mean when it says we should hate evil? "Hate" is the opposite of "love", so it means that we are repulsed by things that are wrong. We do not embrace them, and certainly do not want them in our lives. When God was describing Job to the devil, He referred to him as "A blameless and upright man, one who fears God and shuns evil." (Job 1:8). According to God, Job was someone who feared Him. He was also a man who shunned evil.

WISDOM, AND THE FEAR OF THE LORD

We may say to ourselves, "I live a good, clean life. I don't commit crimes." That, of course, is very good. However, it brings to mind the story of the rich young ruler. He had kept the commandments from his youth, and we read that Jesus loved him. Sadly though, something was more important to him than having riches in heaven. In his case, it was having riches on earth, and when Jesus challenged him on it, he walked away, sorrowful.

"Evil", therefore, is not only criminal-like behavior, but can involve other things, even things that are socially acceptable. One such area is occult involvement. If we are people who shun evil, we will have nothing to do with things that are so much as tainted by the occult. This includes reading horoscopes, having our fortune told, following superstitions, and having good luck charms, as well as the more obvious occult matters such as séances and ouija boards. Further, if we are people who fear the Lord, who shun evil, we will be careful what we watch and what we read. If some form of entertainment has an occult theme, we will have nothing to do with it. It is not a question of whether that entertainment is enjoyable or fun. If it is tainted with the occult, we have nothing to do with it. Occult things are the enemy's territory, so our love for God is demonstrated by our allegiance to Him and rejection of the tainted things.

To summarize then, the fear of the Lord is to have a deep love and respect for Him. This will be evidenced by our rejecting things that He is opposed to. It will also mean that we obey Him in matters that are not necessarily sin but things that He has asked us to do or not to do. To quote Job again; "I have treasured the words of His mouth more than my necessary food." (Job 23:12). We are to be obedient in all that He asks, not just the things that are appealing to us. We are to treasure His word.

Occasionally, one meets someone who asks, "Is it okay for a Christian to do..." It is as if there is some line where behavior crosses from Christian to non-Christian, and the person wants to know how close they can come without crossing that line. If we have the fear of God in our hearts, our attitude is not how close we can come to the line but how far away we can get. We must not flirt with disobedience or we will never be wise.

Returning to the instruction in the Bible that the fear of the Lord is the beginning of wisdom, we need to consider that this contains an important key to becoming wise people. Having the fear of the Lord is the starting line. This wisdom is the wisdom of God that helps us draw close to Him and to make sound decisions. There is a certain wisdom that some people have, even though they may have no regard for the things of God. For example, some businessmen are very skilled in operating their business and know how to make money. That is a certain wisdom, but we are speaking of the wisdom of God that benefits all aspects of our life.

If we consider a great river, with the vast volume of water flowing to the ocean, it is remarkable that it begins with a trickle of melting snow, high in a mountain. This is the beginning. Similarly, if we are to be blessed with great wisdom, we have to have the right starting point, and this is the fear of the Lord. Without the fear of the Lord, we will never have the wisdom of God.

In concluding our brief study on the fear of the Lord, let us look at some of the benefits. We have already seen that it leads to wisdom, which is sufficient reason alone to purse the fear of the Lord. Some other benefits are:

WISDOM, AND THE FEAR OF THE LORD

- Psalm 25:14. The secret of the Lord is with those who fear Him. God reveals secrets to those who walk close to Him. We see this in the insights given to the Apostle John, who wrote the book of Revelation, where He was shown future events, extending beyond the second coming of Jesus. If we want knowledge and understanding, we must have the fear of the Lord first. God will reveal things to those who truly walk with Him, and to walk with Him we must be compatible.

- Proverbs 22:4. By humility and the fear of the Lord are riches and honor and life. We should point out that riches may or may not refer to material things. There are many riches that are not material, such as the love of a spouse and children, and the abiding presence of God.

- Isaiah 33:6. The fear of the Lord is His treasure. What a wonderful promise. God has treasure for us, and His treasure exceeds the treasures of this world. When we pass on from this life, we will take with us our character and our relationship with God. We cannot take the material treasures. And God says that His treasure is the fear of the Lord. It is a priceless gift that He wants us to have.

- Psalm 128:1. Blessed is everyone who fears the Lord. There is a blessing for every person who walks in the fear of the Lord, and God's blessings are very wonderful indeed.

INTENDED FOR GREATNESS

God has given us a tremendous incentive to know the fear of the Lord in our lives, and thereby to become wise people. However, He has also given us a free will, the ability and right to choose our own path. May we be people who desire to know the fear of the Lord with all our hearts. That is what is best for us.

SEVEN

STAYING ON COURSE

We have seen that Solomon was a man who began his adult life very well, but stumbled in his later years. From the time that he was a young man, God blessed him with extraordinary wisdom, understanding, and wealth. He became the premier ruler of the nations of his day, and his favor and understanding were sought after by the peoples of those other nations. He had inherited a kingdom ruled over by his father David, who was an immensely popular king and a true man of God. God loved Solomon too, calling him Jedidiah, which means, "friend of God." Certainly, Solomon had it all going for him, as we would say.

Perhaps we will not have such a spiritual fall as Solomon did, but we have to realize that we are human, just as he was, and therefore susceptible to temptations and less than optimal decisions. Obviously, we want to avoid a fall and be people who are faithful to the Lord for all of our lives. It would appear that Solomon returned to the Lord before he died, and that is very important. However, he must have wasted many years in the time when he fell away.

In any kind of contest, the final result is what matters. There may be interest in how the game or race has progressed, but what everyone wants to know is the outcome. Who won? I recall that, when living in New Zealand, I was excited when two of the country's athletes won gold medals in Olympic races for 800 meters and 5,000 meters, only about an hour apart. However, if you were to ask me who was leading either race at the half-way point, or even going into the last lap, I could not tell you. I don't even recall where the New Zealand athletes were placed as they turned into the final straight, racing toward the tape. Does that matter? Not at all. But I know who won.

So it is in life. How we are at various ages and stages in life does indeed matter, because just like in a race, it positions us for things that God has in our future. In the 5,000 meter race that I mentioned, the eventual winner intentionally dropped to last place for the first lap in order to avoid the jostling and possibly being spiked, as the field settled into the race. Perhaps it was an important decision that enabled him to eventually win. It is hard to know, but it was his tactics, and the tactics were planned for winning. I have observed that as we walk with God, one thing builds upon another, and frequently, our involvement in something at some point in our life prepares us for some other task that God has for us later. It seems that nothing is wasted, even the times when we stumble.

I have known a man who, prior to meeting the Lord around the age of forty, had lived a life of violent crime since his early teens. He had spent approximately half of his life in various jails, including some years in a prison intended for hard-core criminals. Some years later, having been released on parole, he began to work with young people, particularly teenagers. When he spoke, everyone listened. Intently. And the story of his prior life was instrumental in leading hundreds of these teenagers to the Lord, no doubt saving many of them from making shipwreck of their own lives. Those first forty years, which had been so destructive, now became extremely productive as the Lord harnessed this man and caused the story of those terrible years to be instrumental in saving many others. Yes, when we walk with the Lord, nothing is wasted, not even our failures.

Of course, we should not approach life with a plan to initially make a mess of things and later stage a miraculous comeback. This is foolish thinking. We should not intentionally waste our years, and we don't even know if God will grant us that opportunity for a comeback. Solomon himself wrote "If a tree falls to the south or the north, in the place where the tree falls, there it shall lie" (Ecclesiastes 11:3). In other words, there comes a time when no more can be done. Nothing can be reversed, and there is no opportunity to remedy past mistakes. When a tree falls, it no longer moves. It remains where it has fallen. We want our finish to be strong, not regretful.

There are examples in the Bible of people who started poorly but finished well, and vice-versa. The apostle Paul is one such example. His life was characterized by zeal, but in his early years, that zeal was horribly misplaced. He was the chief persecutor of the church and responsible for many Christians being beaten, imprisoned, and killed. Their punishments had nothing to do with real crimes, or behavior that was detrimental to society. It was all because they were Christians.

However, the Lord met Paul one day while traveling to Damascus to extend his persecutions to Christians in that city. From that point until the end of his life, Paul was completely changed. He became the main apostle to the Gentiles, founding many churches. His letters to those churches now comprise a significant portion of the New Testament. Late in his life, and knowing that he would soon be executed for his faith, Paul was able to write to Timothy, saying, "I have fought the good fight, I have finished the race, I have kept the faith." (2 Timothy 4:7). A man who started so badly, finished superbly, right to his last breath.

The apostle Peter also knew what it was to fall and recover. On the way to the Mount of Olives, just hours before His arrest, Jesus told His disciples that they would stumble because of Him. Peter replied that regardless of the others, he would never do so (Matthew 26:31-33). We know that Peter did in fact deny the Lord three times and had to be restored by the Lord. He had great confidence in his own abilities and did not appreciate how character flaws can cause us to stumble.

Peter certainly learned from this experience. He became the leading apostle and was faithful to the Lord throughout the remainder of his life. In the second of his letters, he listed eight qualities that we need to develop in our lives, and said that "… if you do these things you will never stumble." (2 Peter 1:10). Not only had Peter recovered, but he was able to show others how not to repeat his earlier failing.

There are other examples in the Bible of people who recovered from a fall. David and Moses are two who readily come to mind. They serve as examples to us of the grace of God in granting a second chance, and all of those we have mentioned finished their lives strong in the Lord, serving Him faithfully to the end. This is how we also should be, but how much better to be faithful throughout than to need to recover from a fall.

Unfortunately, there are also examples of others who did not recover from their failing. Judas Iscariot is certainly one such example. He betrayed the Lord, providing the Pharisees with the assistance that they desperately needed in order to successfully arrest Jesus without causing an uproar amongst the people. Judas later realized that he had erred, and returned the money that he had been paid. However, there was no way back for him, and he committed suicide. A man whose name should be inscribed on the foundations of the wall of the New Jerusalem (Revelation 21:14) instead awaits a terrible fate (Matthew 26:24).

Another example is a man named Demas. He traveled with Paul and is mentioned in some of Paul's letters. For example, in Philemon 1:24, Paul refers to Demas, Luke, and others as his "fellow laborers." Paul was not an easy man to please, and Demas must have been one who made a strong impression for his service to the Lord. Later however, Demas was to leave Paul. In 2 Timothy 4:10 we read, "Demas has forsaken me, having loved this present world."

We should pay attention to the example of Demas. For many years, he could only be described as a committed, on-fire Christian. However, there must have been something in his heart that was not surrendered to the Lord, which in time turned him aside. We need to be humble, knowing that we too have the propensity to stumble. We must ask the Lord to cause us to see our weak areas and to give us grace to overcome.

Jesus frequently used parables when teaching, creating stories from scenes that were typical in His day to illustrate truths. One of the better known parables is the Parable of the Talents

(Matthew 25:14-30). In this parable, a man leaves sums of money with his servants for them to invest while he is away. To one he gave five talents, and to another he gave ten talents. Both of them doubled their investment, and both were commended as being "good and faithful." However, a third servant, who was given just one talent, did not invest it at all. Instead, he buried it to keep it safe for when his master returned. The master was angry and called him a wicked and lazy servant, took his talent from him, and cast him into outer darkness.

The parable depicts the fact that we do not all have the same talents or abilities. Some of us seem to be able to do almost anything, some have lesser skills, and some of us have just one or a few things that we do well. The parable seems to show that the greatest danger in not utilizing our abilities lies with those of us who are not as gifted as others. Perhaps we have a tendency to look at the more gifted Christians and say to ourselves that we really can't make much of a contribution because we are not nearly as talented as they are. We compare ourselves to others and come up short, and fail to utilize what we have for the kingdom of God.

It is obvious from the parable that Jesus expects us to use the abilities that He has given to us. It is also obvious that we are not created equal when it comes to abilities. However, the commendation that Jesus gave to the man with five talents was the same as for the man with ten talents. The man with five did not have to perform as if he had ten…he just had to utilize what he had been given.

Another interesting point is that when the master took the one talent away from the servant to whom he had initially given it, he gave it to the servant who already had the most talents. In our somewhat socialistic thinking, we would have given it to the man with five to help to equalize the abilities of these two good servants. However, by giving it to the servant who already had ten, Jesus illustrated that as we utilize the gifts that He has given to us, we will receive more. As we consider this parable in the context of staying on course and finishing our life well, we see that it behooves us to continually seek to use our gifts, and to continually be pressing on for a closer walk with the Lord.

EIGHT

SOLOMON AND DAVID

Solomon was a son of David and Bathsheba, and he succeeded his father to the throne of Israel. His parents were of great influence in his early life, and it would seem from the book of Proverbs that they spent considerable time training him for the task of leading the nation.

Solomon had as good a start to his life and kingship as anyone could imagine. Consider these facts:

- His father was a great man of God, and is still revered today. God described David as being a man after His own heart, an extremely high compliment indeed. This was the man who instructed Solomon, so the latter would have been well-versed in understanding the ways of God.

- David had fought many wars and captured the full territory that God had promised the children of Israel. This meant that Solomon inherited a kingdom that was at peace, and superior to the regions around him.

- Because of the reputation of David, Solomon would have been respected from the outset. He would not have had to establish himself in the eyes of the people to the same degree as would a relative stranger.

- God Himself appeared to Solomon shortly after he came to the throne. This is a privilege that is not granted to many people. In fact, He later appeared to Solomon a second time as well.

- When God appeared to Solomon, He promised him wealth, wisdom, understanding, and favor with the surrounding nations. This was an amazing start to his reign, and these blessings would ensure that he could succeed beyond the measure of other kings.

Without a doubt, Solomon was destined for greatness, and it would have appeared that he could not fail. However, in all of His wonderful preparations, one thing was missing, something that had certainly been part of David's life. It is something that is integral to our maturity as people and as people of God.

Solomon had not been tried.

When David rose to prominence after defeating Goliath, he quickly became the darling to the people. This provoked jealousy in the heart of King Saul. When Samuel told Saul that he had been rejected by God and that his kingdom would not pass to his descendants, but rather to a man that God would choose, Saul sought to kill David. Saul had correctly deduced that David was the man that Samuel referred to, and the obvious way to prevent him from becoming king was to kill him. This, of course, does not speak well of Saul. Perhaps if he had humbled himself and repented of his disobedience, his end would have been very different. Based on the character of God, I believe so.

It is a principle of life that we will all be tried. Adam and Eve were tested on obedience regarding the tree of the knowledge of good and evil. Abraham was tried regarding his faith in God's promise. Similarly, so was Joseph. Queen Esther was tried as to whether she regarded her own safety above that of the Jewish people. And of course, David spent several years on the run, hiding from his father-in-law, Saul, who had all of the resources of the kingdom at his disposal to apprehend him.

In these years, we see examples of why David was regarded so highly by God. One point was his willingness to receive others who came to join him. The larger the band, the more difficult it would be to hide, and the greater the need for provisions to sustain them, yet David allowed them to join him. It is not as if they were the kind of individuals that one would seek out for one's band of men either, because other than his family, they are described as being "everyone who was in debt, and everyone who was in distress, and everyone who was discontented" (1 Samuel 22:3). In all, there were about four hundred men, so the total number would have been considerably larger with the inclusion of women and children.

Another point that particularly revealed the heart of David was his sparing the life of Saul, not once but twice. He could have killed Saul and ended his difficulties, and who would have blamed him? Surely the people would have perceived that God delivered Saul to him, just like his men said in the cave (1 Samuel 24:4). However, David was a man after God's heart. Saul had not inherited the throne, nor had he taken it by violence. He had been appointed by God and anointed for the task by Samuel the prophet. Regardless of the impact upon himself, David spared Saul because of his respect for God. In the end, God did remove Saul, and David came to the throne with an unblemished reputation, one that no one could question. This was to be essential to uniting the entire nation under his leadership.

I had an incident concerning sparing someone in my own life. My boss had been doing some things that, while not illegal, were certainly not right. He was misleading the parent company as to our financial profitability, and if discovered, his deception could potentially lead to his dismissal. When it began to collapse around him, he accused me of causing the problem. Actually, I was not in a position to do what I had been accused of doing, but that did not stop him from accusing me because he needed a scapegoat. A few months later, I was presented with a perfect opportunity to expose him and to vindicate myself. A lady from the corporate office was visiting on another matter and in the course of discussing it, she asked me a question. The answer would have revealed what my boss had been doing. I can't recall how I answered, but I know that I avoided a straight answer, and the conversation moved on.

I'm sure we have all had experiences when many thoughts rapidly flash through our mind in just a second or two. This happened to me when the lady asked that question, but the words that came clearly to me were, "He is not going to come down by my hand." That is why I avoided answering the question, and passed on an opportunity to exact revenge on him. However, God says that vengeance is His, and just a few months later, my boss was dismissed from the company over another matter. On the other hand, I continued to work there for many years and enjoyed an excellent reputation, so much so that the company asked me to continue to work on a part-time basis after I officially retired. I suppose this incident when I was falsely accused was a test to see if I could qualify for other things that God intended for me, and it is true that not too long after this, I entered into a period of significant spiritual growth. Like David, I had spared a man who was over me and had treated me unjustly, and it was a sobering realization that God removed him.

Returning to Solomon, this man inherited a wonderful situation, but he was not tried beforehand. His trials came later, and he did not perform well, as we know. We really don't like trials. They are not fun. However, the apostle James instructs us to be grateful because of the benefits that we receive from them (James 1:2-5). Our coming through our trials with our character and attitudes intact and hopefully improved is vital to our developing a close walk with the Lord. Often, it is essential to our fulfilling the work that God has for us.

Our relationship with God is demonstrated by certain things, one of which is our trust in Him. As we come to know Him better, we trust Him more. We understand His character, and we know that He is not just the mighty, all-powerful creator and upholder of the universe, but also a wonderful friend who truly loves us. Trusting God is not something that comes naturally to us. This is because we cannot see Him, and because He is not some sort of genie whose job is to fulfill all of our requests. Certainly, God does answer prayer, but His ways are not ours, and so when He does what He has determined to be the best course of action, it may not correspond to what we would like. God sees a bigger picture than us.

Perhaps the fundamental reason why trust does not come easily to us though, is because our attitudes are self-centered. We are primarily concerned about how a situation affects us, rather than what would bring honor to Him.

Trust is actually quite fragile, which is why we have to be diligent in our relationships to ensure that we guard the trust that others place in us. In our relationship with God, when things do not work out the way we think they should, our trust in Him may be damaged if we regard Him in human terms. If something happens, some hard or even tragic event, how will we respond? We may ask, "Why have I had to go through so much grief?" "God could have spared me this pain, why didn't He step in?" Because of the hardship that we have endured, the logical conclusion then, is that we can't trust Him. And therefore, we back away from things related to God, such as attending church, praying, reading the Bible, and perhaps even forsaking a righteous life to some degree. However, we are looking at what happened in terms of how it affected us. We have not considered what might be the plan of God, or perhaps how He may have spared us and/or others some greater grief.

The truth is that there are many things that happen in life where we can't comprehend why they happened the way that they did. Unfortunately, a lack of understanding of His beautiful nature will lead us to a wrong conclusion and cause us to mistrust the One who demonstrated a love beyond measure when Jesus died for us. It is so important that we have a proper understanding of the nature and character of God. In life, we will face difficult things, and blaming God for them is the wrong response.

Let us consider the difficulties that David had to face, some of which were of his own making, but difficult trials nevertheless:

- When King Saul set a dowry for David to marry his daughter, he secretly hoped that David would be killed while fulfilling it.

- On two occasions, Saul tried to kill him with a spear.

- David had to leave his wife when he fled for his life.

- His father-in-law gave his wife to another man.

- For several years, David was a fugitive in the Judean wilderness while Saul hunted him to kill him.

- Although he saved the city of Keilah from the Philistines, the city intended to betray him to Saul.

- A band of Amalekites captured the wives and children of David and his men, and burned their city. Their grief was so great that they wept until they had no more strength to weep. As if this was not bad enough, the men talked of killing David because of it.

- He suffered the public humiliation and disgrace from his adultery with Bathsheba and for arranging the death of her husband.

- His son from his adultery died after a few days.

- It is likely that his second son also died while still a young man.

- His oldest son raped his daughter.

- His third son murdered his oldest son in vengeance.

- The third son for a time succeeded in driving David from Jerusalem, usurping the throne.

- He endured cursing from one of his citizens and being pelted with rocks.

- His close friend and counsellor betrayed him.

- The northern tribes rebelled against him for a period.

- He experienced a plague in the nation in which 70,000 men died.

- Shortly before his death, his fourth son attempted to take the throne that he had promised to Solomon.

- In his late sixties, this mighty, strong warrior developed health issues such that his body would not stay warm.

In addition, when we read the Psalms, we find many references to David being oppressed by enemies, lamenting about being falsely accused, and other difficulties. The Psalms also reveal his great love for God, his trust in and commitment to Him, and praise and thanksgiving for His mercies. Through all of these trails and difficult situations, David never faltered. He knew the nature of God. There must have been times when he wondered when it would all end, and how it would end, but he never lost his faith and trust in God.

As we conclude our comparison of David and Solomon, let us allow them to show us the essential difference of their innermost heart from their own words. David said, "One thing I ask from the Lord, this only do I seek; that I may dwell in the house of the Lord all the days of my life, to gaze on the beauty of the Lord and to seek Him in His temple" (Psalm 27:4). David was a man who loved God above all other things in his life. He desired the presence of God more than anything, and he saw the Lord as someone he could best describe as beautiful. David knew the Lord, and although he committed a grievous sin, he never forsook the Him.

Solomon, however, had a different perspective. He certainly understood spiritual principles, and was remorseful of his sin. In his heart however, he also loved excessive behavior.

INTENDED FOR GREATNESS

When he was an older man, looking back on his life, he said, "Whatever my eyes desired I did not keep from them. I did not withhold my heart from any pleasure." (Ecclesiastes 2:10). Solomon did not measure up to his father's character, and unfortunately, the testimony of the Bible regarding him is that, "his heart was not loyal to the Lord his God, as was the heart of his father David." (1 Kings 11:4). The hearts of the two men were different, and how they are remembered is also different.

NINE

SOLOMON'S LEGACY

Solomon's legacy is one of extremes. There are some things that are very good, and some that are very bad. When he died, the kingdom was well respected. Solomon had accumulated great wealth and valuable trading operations were in place. The country was prosperous and essentially at peace with other nations. Solomon had engaged in substantial construction projects, the best known being the temple. This temple was magnificent. It has been estimated that the value of the silver and gold used in its construction in today's money exceeded $80 billion, let alone the cost of cedar, other materials, and labor. God blessed the temple at its dedication with His own presence in such measure that the priests were not able to minister because of the glory of God. Had he done nothing else, Solomon would always have been remembered for the temple that he built.

Solomon had been a teacher, not only of his own people but also of other peoples who came to learn from him. His wisdom set Israel apart. He had spoken 3,000 proverbs and written 1,005 songs (1 Kings 4:32). He also wrote the books of Ecclesiastes and Song of Solomon in the Bible, and much of the book of Proverbs. Solomon was certainly not lazy, and used the talents that God had given to him to the fullest. He was prolific in his undertakings and achievements.

When historians consider greatness, Solomon has few peers. His abilities and accomplishments exceed most other leaders. However, when we are considering greatness there is an aspect that tends to be overlooked, and that is character. We will look at certain leaders, perhaps political or military, and say that this person was great because we focus on their achievements. However, God focuses on character.

An example is Alexander the Great. His actual name was Alexander III of Macedon, a king of Greece who embarked on an unprecedented military campaign, such that by the age of thirty he had created one of the largest empires in history. He was undefeated in battle. Why do we consider him great? Because of his astonishing military accomplishments. He was a superb tactician, courageous, and a strong leader of men. However, he was also a brutal, domineering man with a serious drinking problem, which probably led to his death. Alexander was great in the eyes of man, but in the eyes of God, he failed.

After an outstanding beginning to his reign, when he humbly asked God for wisdom to govern His people, Solomon later led the country into idolatry. Sometimes we wonder how people can do certain things, and such is the case here. God had appeared to Solomon on two occasions, given him wonderful promises, and proceeded to bless him, just as He had promised.

After being blessed so wonderfully, it is hard to fathom why Solomon would forsake the Lord to worship idols. The root cause, of course, lay in his excessive behaviors and disobedience to God's word.

The consequences of Solomon's disobedience were very significant. The kingdom was divided, the northern tribes coming under the rule of Jeroboam, and the southern tribes under the rule of Solomon's son, Rehoboam. This is an important although unenviable aspect of his legacy, the dividing of the nation. In time, it would lead to war between the two kingdoms. Essentially, this amounted to civil war, which was really tragic, because in it, people of the same heritage and national affiliation fought and killed each other. It was Rehoboam's poor decision that triggered the split, but the root cause lay with Solomon's disobedience.

We might ask ourselves, what did Solomon really think of life, and God, and mankind's responsibilities? We can find the answer in his own writings, and it provides a guide that we should follow. Late in his life, Solomon wrote the book of Ecclesiastes, which begins with the statement, "Vanity, vanity, all is vanity," (Ecclesiastes 1:2). This is a translation of the Hebrew word "hebel" which means "vapor" or "breath", pointing to something being fleeting, temporary, and hard to grasp.

Solomon understood that life is short, and that there are things about life that are difficult for us to understand. He describes how in his search for meaning, he looked to pleasure, work, and intellectual evaluation, but nothing satisfied his soul or answered all his questions.

After all his experimentation and reasoning, struggling to understand meaning in life, Solomon closed his book by saying, "Let us hear the conclusion of the whole matter: Fear God and keep His commandments, for this is man's all." (Ecclesiastes 12:13). Solomon had correctly concluded that things can be hard to understand if we look only from the perspective of our temporary life on earth. Ultimately, meaning is found in a relationship with the eternal God who created us, trusting in Him who understands what we may not.

Solomon's conclusion is particularly relevant because he was not parroting something that he had heard another person say, nor was he saying what he believed he was supposed to say because he was the king of God's people. What he wrote came after a thorough search for meaning in life, utilizing the extensive wisdom that God had given to him. After all this, his conclusion was that if we want the best for ourselves in life, we should walk with God, honor Him, and be obedient to His commands for us. And so we should.

www.ingramcontent.com/pod-product-compliance
Lightning Source LLC
Chambersburg PA
CBHW070438010526
44118CB00014B/2093